Reader's Digest **READING SKILL BUILDER**

SILVER EDITION EDITORS

Miriam Weiss Meyer and Peter Travers, Project Editors

Barbara Antonopulos and Jacqueline Kinghorn, Editors

SILVER EDITION CONSULTANTS

Fred Chavez, Director of Programs
Los Angeles City Reading Support Services Center
Los Angeles, California

Marguerite E. Fuller, Assistant Supervisor of Language Arts
Norwalk Public Schools
Norwalk, Connecticut

Sister Maria Loyola, I.H.M.,Chairperson, Reading Curriculum Committee
Archdiocese of Philadelphia
Philadelphia, Pennsylvania

Dr. John. F. Savage, Coordinator, Reading Specialist Program
Boston College, School of Education
Chestnut Hill, Massachusetts

Richard B. Solymos, Reading Resource Teacher
School Board of Broward County
Fort Lauderdale, Florida

READER'S DIGEST EDUCATIONAL DIVISION
© 1977 by Reader's Digest Services, Inc., Pleasantville, N.Y. 10570. All rights reserved, including
the right to reproduce this book or parts thereof in any form.
Reader's Digest ® Trademark Reg. U.S. Pat. Off. Marca Registrada ISBN 0-88300-412-7
Printed in the United States of America.

■ ■ ■ **Part 2**

Silver Edition

STORIES

4  **Have Some Rally!** 🔊
Gerald learns what the word *rally* means when fire nearly destroys his parents' ranch. RDX 109

14 **Library with a Split Nationality**
One half of this library is in Canada, and the other half is in the United States. RDX 110

20 **Spiders—Eight-Legged Wonders of the World**
Take a close-up look at spiders. RDX 111

28 **Dental Dean**
Going to the dentist is never scary when the dentist is Juliann Bluitt. RDX 112

34  **The Giant Lunch Box** 🔊
When Mr. Tozzi sent Polly to the school cafeteria to get lunch for the class, he never counted on the new sandwich-making machine. RDX 113

42 **Coyote!**
Are coyotes good or bad? Jenny found the answer when a coyote and its pups made their den on her grandfather's ranch. RDX 114

🔊 Stories for which Audio Lessons are available.
RDX number indicates RDX card for that story.

52 | **Brave Journey**
Alain Bombard spent 52 days in a rubber raft to prove that people <u>can</u> survive a shipwreck if they use the simple things around them. RDX 115

62 | **They Take Snapshots in Sound**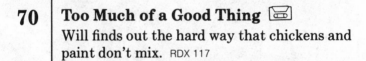
Dick Kenny's nickname is the Crazy Tapeworm. He and others like him are busy right now recording sounds.
RDX 116

70 | **Too Much of a Good Thing**
Will finds out the hard way that chickens and paint don't mix. RDX 117

76 | **Fish Pictures**
Learn the Japanese art of *Gyotaku,* or fish printing. RDX 118

82 |

Cowhands of the Deep
Underwater cowhands who herd fish are only part of what may be in store for us in the future.
RDX 119

88 | **And She Brought Them Light**
Dorothea Dix fought a one-person battle to have mentally ill people treated like human beings. RDX 120

Have

New Mexico got plenty of rain that spring. Grass grew high and thick. It could be made into food for cattle. My parents' hopes rose, too. Now they wouldn't have to buy food for our cattle. They could use that money to pay off old bills instead.

One day Dad drove into town to sell some of our calves. Before he left, he told us, "I'll buy a pair of boots, too. I'll be back tomorrow with them on."

4

Some Rally!

by Gerald Moore

The next day, Mom, my younger sister
and I went to church. On our way home,
Mom stared down the road. "Do you see
smoke, Gerald? Hang on, children!"

Mom pressed down on the gas pedal. Our
pickup truck leaped forward and shot down
our dirt lane.

She did not mention the things we all feared. A big fire could burn up all the grass we needed for our cattle. It might also burn our ranch house to the ground.

We could see the smoke clearly now, for it hid the mountains and turned the sky black. Mom slammed on the brakes in front of the gate, and I hopped out to open it.

"Leave it open!"

I did what she told me, but I was scared. We <u>never</u> left gates open.

Mom drove past the house. Then she cried, "Oh, no!" In front of us, a wall of yellow flames ate the high grass. A brisk wind

6

pushed them toward us. Three cows raced ahead of the fire.

Mom turned back to the house. She raced for the phone to call for help. Our neighbors came quickly. Even though they were dressed in their best church clothes, they came to fight the fire.

Mom shouted, "Gerald, run to the barn. Get all the cloth sacks you can find."

I raced to the barn and grabbed them. Someone started pumping water to soak the sacks in. We lived too far from water to use the town fire engines. Our only weapons would be wet sacks.

The grown-ups snatched up the thick sacks and formed a thin line at the edge of the

fire. They whipped the ground with their wet sacks, trying to beat out the flames, while we older children carried water in buckets and soaked the sacks.

Finally Dad got home. When he saw the blaze, he remembered something. "There's a big, empty water tank on the old truck. Fill it up with well water—on the double!"

For a while, I thought the fire would win. Gusts of wind pushed it toward the house, but the neighbors worked harder, beating out flames.

Then the wind shifted. The fire raced toward the road, away from the house. The road stopped the fire from going any farther. The flames died down, and the neighbors beat them out.

By dark the fire was gone. The grass we had been depending on to feed our cattle was gone, too. Now there would be no extra money to help pay bills and buy things we needed. We would have to search for the

cattle that had run away. All of our hopes burned up that afternoon.

Dad and Mom stayed outside, shaking hands with all the neighbors. After they thanked our friends for their aid and said good-bye, we all went inside to the kitchen. Mom and Dad sank into chairs. "I'll get you some coffee," I said. Their faces were streaked with soot, and their shoulders were slumped. I wanted to cry for all we had lost—the cattle, the grass, the dreams.

"Dad, you've ruined your new boots!" I gasped. Dad's wonderful new boots were wet and scuffed.

"Don't worry, son. They'll make good work boots, for we'll have lots of work to do."

"You can have the money I've been saving, Dad, if that will help."

"You keep that money, Gerald. You'll need it for a trip around the world someday."

"Around the world?" I didn't understand what he meant.

"Sure. All young people take a trip around the world. I did."

"Did you really, Dad?"

"Ask your mother. She wouldn't have married anybody who hadn't been around the world." Dad started to grin, and Mom laughed at his words. Suddenly we all laughed.

We forgot the fire for a minute, and we laughed over Dad's joke.

Mom hugged Dad hard. She said softly, "You have more rally than an army, Ben."

I didn't know what the word *rally* meant until then. Our family had rally. We had lost most of the ranch that day, and we could still laugh. Even a fire couldn't make us give up. I knew rally was worth having.

RANCH TALK *sentence meaning*

The sentences below contain word groups which are written in slanted letters. Write the numerals of their meanings in the blanks.

Meanings
1. as fast as possible
2. sped; raced
3. depended upon; needed

Sentences
____ The grass we had *counted on* to feed our cattle was gone, too.
____ Our pickup truck leaped forward and *shot down* our dirt lane.
____ Fill it up with well water—*on the double.*

↜54 · *Best Score 3 · My Score* ____

THE WHOLE PICTURE *generalizations*

Check (✔) the four statements that would be true of the Moore family.

____ 1. They have a lot of money.
____ 2. They love each other.
____ 3. They work hard.
____ 4. Their neighbors don't like them.
____ 5. They live far from town.
____ 6. They have rally.

↜122 · *Best Score 4 · My Score* ____

AFTER THE FIRE *inferences*

Check (✔) the three things that the Moore family would probably do after the fire.

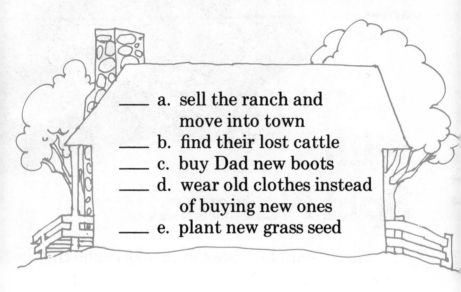

_____ a. sell the ranch and move into town

_____ b. find their lost cattle

_____ c. buy Dad new boots

_____ d. wear old clothes instead of buying new ones

_____ e. plant new grass seed

73 • Best Score 3 • My Score _____
All Best Scores 10 • All My Scores _____

HAVING RALLY *comparison/contrast*

Rally helped the Moore family overcome their problems. Tell how. Then tell about a time when you or someone you know has had rally.

Key Words
library
nationality
government
arrest
border

Library with a Split Nationality

The woman browsing for books inside the library was doing what a lot of other people do there. She was crossing back and forth from Canada to the United States without having either government stop her.

The library? The Haskell Free Library and Opera House. The place? Well, not one place, but two. The library is set on the dividing line between Canada and the United States. One half of the building is located in Derby Line, Vermont. The other half is in Rock Island, Quebec.

14

by William E. Pauli

The Haskell Library isn't a mapmaker's mistake. In 1901 the Haskell family of Derby Line had the building erected for the free use of both towns. The opera house rarely opens now. But it isn't really an opera house. Actually it's a theater on the second and third floors of the building. The ground floor houses the library.

In the days when the opera house was open, there was an actor who had committed a crime. The United States government wanted to arrest him. He was on stage when he spotted the U.S. marshals waiting by the

front door to take him in. The actor simply made his exit out the back door to the Canadian side of the border, where the U.S. marshals couldn't arrest him.

The library has had to deal with other problems. The library has to purchase its electricity from a power company in the United States. But this U.S. company gets its electricity from Canada. Phone service is on the Canadian side, so someone in Derby Line who wants to ring up the library has to call long distance.

Even telling time can be difficult. One year, Vermont switched to daylight saving

time. This meant its clocks were set one hour ahead of Quebec's. The library's front door is in Vermont. But its clock is in Canada. So would the library open according to daylight saving time or standard time?

The people who run the library handled this problem in their usual quiet way. They split the difference. They opened and closed the library a half hour earlier. It's that kind of good will that brings together the people of Rock Island, Quebec, and Derby Line, Vermont. The little Haskell Library could teach the countries of the world a lesson about being good neighbors.

LOOK IT UP *skimming*

Circle the numeral of each correct answer.

What is the real name of the library?
1. The Haskell Public Library and Theater
2. The Haskell Free Library and Opera House

What is the name of the town in Canada in which the library is located?
1. Derby Line   2. Rock Island

In what year was the library built?
1. 1910   2. 1901

On which floor is the library found?
1. second floor   2. ground floor

Which country does the back door face?
1. Canada   2. United States

☞ *132 • Best Score 5 • My Score* ____

CROSSING THE BORDER *cause/effect*

Underline the result of each situation.

An actor once made his exit into Canada.
   a. He couldn't be arrested.
   b. He didn't have to pay U.S. taxes.

The library's telephone service is Canadian.
   a. Someone in Vermont has to call the library long distance.

b. Someone in Vermont can't call the library.

Each side told time in a different way.
    a. The library opens and closes a half hour early.
    b. The library uses Vermont's system.

⟜ 43 · Best Score 3 · My Score ____

MORE THAN BOOKS   *main idea*

Check (✔) the two <u>most important</u> ideas.

____ 1. The opera house is really a theater.
____ 2. The Haskell Library has had to face many unusual situations.
____ 3. The library's clock is in Canada.
____ 4. The electricity is bought from the U.S.
____ 5. The Haskell family put up the library.
____ 6. The library has shown how people, and even countries, can work out problems.

⟜ 39 · Best Score 2 · My Score ____
All Best Scores 10 · All My Scores ____

SPLIT YOUR SCHOOL?   *comparison/contrast*

Suppose one half of your school was in the U.S. and the other half in Canada. What problems would your school have to face? How would you solve these problems?

Key Words

wonders
insects
prey
poisonous

Spiders –
Eight-Legged
Wonders of the World

by Ann Moreton

The next time you see a house spider, stop. Don't kill it. Take a closer look, and you will see a truly marvelous creature. The house spider has eight legs and eight eyes. In spite of its many eyes, it can't see very well. However, the house spider has a very good sense of touch.

One of the most interesting things about the house spider is its web. A spider's web is an amazing work of art. The web is thin but strong for its size.

House Spider

Different types of spiders spin different styles of webs. Most spider webs are used for snaring food—namely, insects. In its web, a spider may catch as many as 2000 insects in one year. When a spider feels something in its web, it runs out. Some spiders wrap up their prey and kill it with a poisonous bite. Other spiders bite their prey first and then wrap it up. In either case, a spider sucks an insect dry and leaves just the crusty shell.

Webs have other uses besides trapping prey. Some webs are built to hatch baby spiders, and other webs are just to be lived in. Sometimes spiders spin their silk to swing from one place to the next or to hang in the air.

A Marbled Spider repairing its web.

Wolf Spider—a hunting spider

Not all spiders build webs. Many hunting spiders don't. Unlike the web builders, hunters can see well. They lie in wait for an insect to pass. Then they grab it.

Tarantula—a hunting spider

Fishing Spider

Most people think spiders live only in buildings or in trees and grass. However, spiders can be found in very unusual places. Some live underwater, under stones and deep in caves. Spiders have been found by fishing boats at sea and by airplane pilots in the sky. Spiders have even been found by climbers on Mount Everest, the tallest mountain in the world.

WEB BUILDER OR HUNTER? *classification/outline*

Put A next to the spiders that spin webs and
B next to the ones that are hunters.

___ house spider
___ wolf spider
___ tarantula

☞41 • *Best Score 3* • *My Score* ___

SPINNING SPIDER *sequence*

The steps the spider below needs to take to
capture its prey are listed underneath. Write
the numerals of the steps in the right order in
the spider's web.

1. The spider runs out onto the web.
2. The spider kills the insect with a
   poisonous bite.
3. The spider wraps up its prey.
4. The spider feels something caught in
   its web.
5. The spider sucks the insect dry.

☞165 • *Best Score 5* • *My Score* ___

I LIKE SPIDERS!   *fact/opinion*

Four of the sentences below tell you facts about spiders. The other two sentences tell you how the author feels about spiders. Check (✔) the two sentences that tell you the author's opinion.

_____ 1. Spiders have eight legs and eight eyes.
_____ 2. Not all spiders build webs.
_____ 3. Spiders are found all over the world, from Mount Everest to the sea.
_____ 4. Spiders are marvelous creatures.
_____ 5. Spiders' webs come in many styles.
_____ 6. A spider's web is an amazing work of art.

☞*40 • Best Score 2 • My Score _____*
All Best Scores 10 • All My Scores _____

A SECOND LOOK   *graphics*

Look at the picture of the spiders in the article. Which spider is the ugliest? the most beautiful? the funniest? the scariest? the most unusual? Give reasons.

Key Words

dental, dentistry
dentist, associate dean
clinic

Dental Dean

Dr. Juliann S. Bluitt is an associate dean at Northwestern University's School of Dentistry in Evanston, Illinois. But she became a dentist almost by accident.

Juliann grew up in Washington, D.C. She had always wanted to be an animal doctor. One day she had to go to the dentist to have her teeth straightened.

"I was just a youngster then," she states. "I can recall the methods my dentist used to straighten my teeth. The results were wonderful."

Dr. Bluitt is one of a handful of female dentists in the United States. Less than two percent of all dentists in the nation are women.

As associate dean, Dr. Bluitt has three jobs. She's a dentist. She helps run the dental school. And she's a teacher. There is one thing she wants to do in all three jobs. Dr. Bluitt wants to know what her patients and students are thinking.

Dr. Bluitt is in charge of the dental clinic. There dental students help 10,000 patients a year. Dr. Bluitt has to solve problems that come up in the clinic.

But being dean takes up a lot of time. Dr. Bluitt wishes she had more time for the teaching part of her job. She feels that students, like patients, should be listened to.

"The student today," she says, "really thinks. You give certain facts. Then you listen to how the student feels about those different facts. It is exciting to me to hear those different feelings."

Dr. Bluitt realizes that going to the dentist's office can be scary for people. There's something frightening about all those machines. The dentist may appear to have magical powers. But Dr. Bluitt doesn't want her patients to be afraid.

"The patient has rights. He or she ought

to be informed of what's happening. We know a lot about teeth. But we aren't magicians. And we aren't perfect. The patient is a person, too."

To help children have less fear, she created a coloring book. The book teaches children how to take care of their teeth.

Dr. Bluitt isn't sorry she didn't become an animal doctor. "When my dog is in pain, I am in pain. The tears just run down my face. I can't do a thing."

That's too bad for the dog. But it's lucky for her patients and students. With dentists like Dr. Bluitt, having a tooth filled doesn't seem quite so scary.

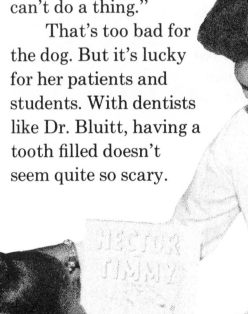

DRILL FOR FACTS *supporting details*

Underline the sentence ending that would help you recall a fact.

1. The word *dentistry* means
    a. a doctor who fixes teeth.
    b. the study and care of teeth.
    c. a place in which a dentist works.

2. To help children be less afraid, Dr. Bluitt
    a. gives them candy.
    b. tells them jokes.
    c. wrote a coloring book about dentistry.

3. The dental students where Dr. Bluitt works
    a. treat 10,000 patients a year.
    b. are all women.
    c. live in New York.

4. Dr. Bluitt wishes she had more time for
    a. shopping.
    b. teaching.
    c. reading.

☞90 · *Best Score 4 · My Score* ____

WHAT DO YOU THINK? *fact/opinion*

Put A before each sentence that is fact. Put B before each sentence that is opinion.

____ Students, like patients, should be listened to.

_____ Dr. Bluitt is an associate dean at Northwestern University's School of Dentistry.

_____ The dentist seems to have magic power.

☞42 • Best Score 3 • My Score _____

FILL IN THE MEANING   *phrase meaning*

Write A before each phrase that tells <u>how</u>.
Write B before each phrase that tells <u>what</u>.
Write C before each phrase that tells <u>where</u>.

_____ by accident
_____ coloring book
_____ Washington, D.C.

☞49 • Best Score 3 • My Score _____
All Best Scores 10 • All My Scores _____

MULL IT OVER   *characterization*

Do you think Dr. Bluitt is a person who cares? Give examples from the article that show why or why not.

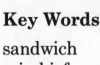

Key Words

sandwich
mischief
salami
bologna
miniature

The Giant Lunch Box

by Sally Berke

"It's almost lunchtime!" said Mr. Tozzi.
"Who wants to get the sandwiches from the
cafeteria?" Hands popped into the air.
Everyone enjoyed going to the lunchroom.

"Polly, you may get the sandwiches for
the class. But please don't get into mischief
today."

Polly sprang to her feet. Mr. Tozzi collected lunch money from each student. He gave Polly the coins and said, "We'll need 15 sandwiches today."

Polly marched down the hall. She loved going to the lunchroom, where she always found something fun to examine. Her curiosity made it difficult for her to stay out of trouble, though. One day Polly played with the knobs on the drinking fountain and almost flooded the hall. Another time she secretly followed the janitor and got lost in the school basement.

Today Polly saw something odd in the lunchroom. There was a huge machine with lots of buttons and a big window. Through the window, Polly saw hundreds of little plastic bags of food. There were packets of

salami, bologna, chicken and turkey. There
were tomatoes, ham, cheese and pickles.
There were eggs, mustard, catsup and salt.
There were many kinds of bread and rolls.

Polly's eyes widened as she gazed into the miniature supermarket. A lunchroom worker walked over to Polly and said, "How do you like our Giant Lunch Box? It just arrived today."

Polly asked, "How does it work?"

The lunchroom worker pointed. "Just put your coins in and press the buttons. Choose your bread and your 'fixings' and make any sort of sandwich you like."

Polly said, "Wow, it's a giant sandwich maker. There must be a million types of sandwiches it can make." Then Polly got an idea. She reached into her pocket for the class lunch money. She began inserting the coins in the machine. First she got several slices of bread. Then she got bags of ham, cheese, turkey, salami, bologna, pickles, eggs, catsup and mustard.

When Polly returned to the classroom, she stood in the doorway with her back to the class. "Polly!" said Mr. Tozzi. "What took you so long? Did you bring back our 15 sandwiches?"

"Not exactly," said Polly. "But I have one sandwich big enough for 15 people."

MAKE YOUR CHOICE *supporting details*

Three endings are given to each sentence below. Draw a line under the one ending that is right.

Polly was sent to the lunchroom to
    a. buy sandwiches.
    b. talk to a lunchroom worker.
    c. deliver a note.

The new machine was called the Giant Lunch Box because
    a. it sold giant-sized food.
    b. Polly made up that name.
    c. it held many kinds of food.

A person using the machine could
    a. get a free lunch.
    b. cook food.
    c. make any kind of sandwich.

Polly returned to the classroom with
    a. 15 sandwiches.
    b. one giant sandwich.
    c. no food.

☞89 • *Best Score 4* • *My Score* _____

GET THE PICTURE *figurative language*

Which sentences did the author use to give you a picture of what happened? Put the numerals in the blanks.

40

Author's Sentences

1. Polly's eyes widened as she gazed into the machine.
2. Polly sprang to her feet.
3. Hands popped into the air.

What Happened?

____ Many students wanted to go for food.

____ Polly stood up.

____ Polly looked at all the food.

☞54 • *Best Score 3* • *My Score* ____

POLLY! *characterization*

Check (✔) three sentences that tell you Polly often got into trouble.

____ 1. Polly secretly followed the janitor.

____ 2. Polly loved going to the lunchroom.

____ 3. Polly returned to the classroom.

____ 4. Polly marched down the hall.

____ 5. Polly played with the knobs on the drinking fountain.

____ 6. Polly liked to find things to examine.

☞82 • *Best Score 3* • *My Score* ____

All Best Scores 10 • *All My Scores* ____

A GIANT SANDWICH *prediction*

What do you think the class did with the giant sandwich? What would you have done?

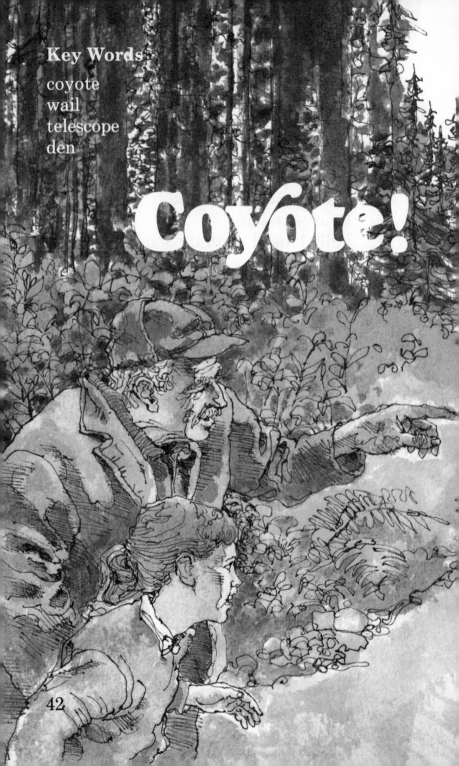

Key Words

coyote
wail
telescope
den

Coyote!

"Jenny, look! That's a coyote—a female ready to have pups!" Gramp's soft voice was filled with excitement. "I haven't seen a coyote for 15 years!"

I watched the coyote trot down the road. She looked like a dog with perky ears. "Shall I fetch your gun, Gramp?"

"No, child," Gramp replied. "There's no need for a gun."

When the coyote saw us, she tore across the road and vanished into a clump of trees.

by Kenn Sherwood Roe

"There's no need for a gun," Gramp repeated.

Most ranchers don't agree. They fear coyotes, and they think coyotes kill chickens and lambs.

"Do coyotes really kill chickens and lambs?" I asked.

"Not usually," Gramp said. "Coyotes eat mice and squirrels, so they help stop these pests from destroying our crops. Coyotes usually eat sick or old deer, not healthy ones. They eat rabbits that aren't fast enough to escape."

That night we heard the coyote howl. Her cry rolled down the valley and echoed in the hills. I shivered at the high-pitched wail. "Maybe she's lonely," Gramp said when he heard the howl. "If she lost her mate, she'll have to raise those pups alone."

"If she survives long enough," Gramma said. "The ranchers will begin the search tomorrow."

"What search?" I asked.

"Jenny, the ranchers hate coyotes, so they will try to kill her." Gramma was right. The next morning, two neighbors came to see

Gramp. They wanted him to help
kill the coyote.

"No," said Gramp. "I hate traps and
poison. I will not use them on my land.
Besides, the coyote hasn't done anything."

"There is no good coyote," said one of
the neighbors. "If you don't use traps and
poison, coyotes will hide on your land. They
will come to our ranches to kill our cattle."

"Wait and see," said Gramp. The two
neighbors stormed off without saying good-
bye.

All our neighbors set their traps and
spread poison. Some searched the nearby
farms with hounds.

Every night we waited for the coyote's howl. When it began, Gramp smiled at me. "She's still alive, Jenny! She's still alive!"

In the next month, no one reported any sheep killed, but the search continued. Ranchers put out more poison and traps. Every time I walked the hills, I found dead birds. They must have eaten poison intended for the coyote. Once, I found a fox dead in a trap. Every night Gramp and I waited. When the coyote howled, we smiled.

One day Gramp said mysteriously, "Hop in the car, Jenny." We bumped our way along to a high field where Gramp halted the car. He reached for a telescope in the back. "We'll have to walk now." We walked a little way and then dropped to our hands and knees. We crawled to the edge of a rise.

Gramp pointed. "Over there is the den."

"Den?" I asked.

"The place where she and her pups live," smiled Gramp.

He pointed to the opposite hill. I spotted the den with the telescope, but no pups poked their noses out of the hole. Gramp said he had seen the pups two days before.

I couldn't spot the pups that day or the next. Finally, three days afterward, I sighted the mother carrying a dead squirrel. I watched her check for danger, and then I heard a yip.

Five baby coyotes tumbled out of the den. They greeted their mother and then tore into supper. They looked like brown puppies.

After supper the pups romped—playing tag, nipping and barking. They teased their mother while she rested, but with a bark she sent them into the den. Playtime was over.

For weeks I went back to observe. Often I saw the pups through the telescope. When I didn't, I thought they were sleeping in the den. But one day I saw them come home with their mother. She had been teaching them to hunt. She crouched down, ready to jump, but a puppy tripped her. She punished that pup with a hard nip.

We watched the pups grow and learn. Gramp often said, "Jenny, those coyotes are safe here. It is our special secret." We smiled at night when the mother howled. We had kept her safe.

The neighbors lost no sheep or cattle. As time passed, they stopped their search. They could hear the howls at night. They still blamed Gramp that the coyote was alive.

One day the mother discovered me. I was watching the den with the telescope. She found me hidden in the tall grass. She looked at me and then slowly walked away. She was not afraid. She did not run.

The den was empty after that. The pups never played there again. I could not find them anywhere on the ranch.

I told Gramp the mother had seen me. "Maybe she moved her pups to hide them. Coyotes sometimes leave a den when they have been discovered," Gramp said.

"Maybe she had visited us long enough," I said. "I hope she'll come back."

But she never did. The coyote had raised her pups safely on our ranch. Then it was time to move on.

ANIMAL TRACKS *signals/antecedents*

Match the letter of each sentence with the explanation of its punctuation mark.

Sentences

    a. "Do coyotes really kill chickens and lambs?"

    b. "She's still alive!"

    c. "If you don't use traps and poison, coyotes will hide on your land."

Explanations

    Sentence _____ asks a question.

    Sentence _____ shows excitement.

    Sentence _____ tells you the exact words of one of the ranchers.

☞ *49 · Best Score 3 · My Score* _____

TRAPPING THE CAUSE *cause/effect*

Circle the letter of the sentence that best explains why the event in the story happened.

1. *We smiled at night when the mother howled.*

    a. The coyote's howl sounded funny.

    b. The howl showed the coyote was still alive.

    c. The howl showed that the coyote had been caught.

2. *The two neighbors stormed off without saying good-bye.*
   a. They were scared of the coyote.
   b. They were in a hurry.
   c. Gramp had made them angry.

3. *Every time I walked the hills, I found dead birds.*
   a. Birds had eaten poison.
   b. Ranchers had shot the birds.
   c. The coyote had killed the birds.

☞52 • *Best Score 3* • *My Score* _____

HUNTING THE FACTS   *facts/opinion*

Put A before each fact and B before each opinion.

_____ 1. Coyotes eat mice and squirrels.
_____ 2. Five pups were born.
_____ 3. Coyotes are pests that destroy farms.
_____ 4. The mother coyote was lonely.

☞86 • *Best Score 4* • *My Score* _____
All Best Scores 10 • *All My Scores* _____

STALKING THE WILD   *inferences*

What do you think the coyote pups learned by playing with one another and with their mother? How would their play help them live in the wild? Explain.

Key Words

journey
victims
shipwreck
funnel
exercises

Brave Journey

by Bernard Groslier

The ship was heading through the sea. Suddenly some of the sailors spotted a life raft. In it was a young man proudly waving a small French flag. Captain Finsen called out to him. "Do you need help?"

The man's voice was weak. "No, thank you. But I would like to know the time and where I am. I am Alain Bombard of France."

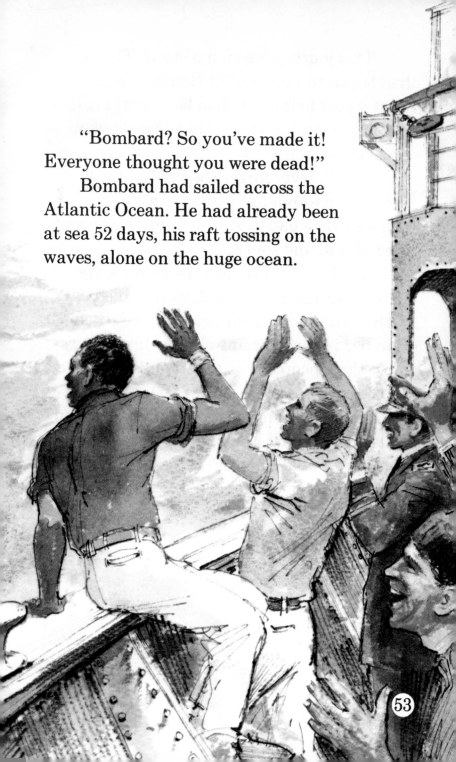

"Bombard? So you've made it! Everyone thought you were dead!"

Bombard had sailed across the Atlantic Ocean. He had already been at sea 52 days, his raft tossing on the waves, alone on the huge ocean.

This journey was not a stunt. The idea had begun to take root in Bombard's mind at least a year before. He had been working in a hospital. One day victims of a shipwreck were brought in.

"I will never forget the sight of those bodies. We weren't able to save a single person. Some had died of drowning. The rest died of cold and shock."

Bombard looked into the records. He found that most shipwreck victims died within three days. Fear helped to kill them. Bombard's task became clear to him. He must show people that they could stay alive on the open seas.

The first needs, of course, were food and water. The young Frenchman found that a person can take small sips of seawater for five or six days—but no longer. Too much salt in

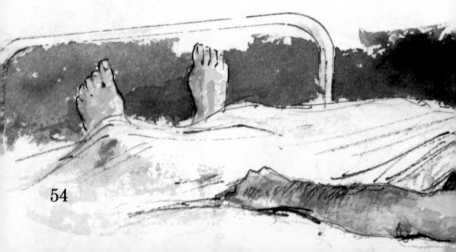

the body will cause death. However, the water in a fish's body is salt-free. So fish were now a source of water as well as of food.

But fish alone couldn't keep a person alive. People need Vitamin C, too. Alain Bombard found this vitamin in *plankton*. Plankton is a floating mass of tiny plants and

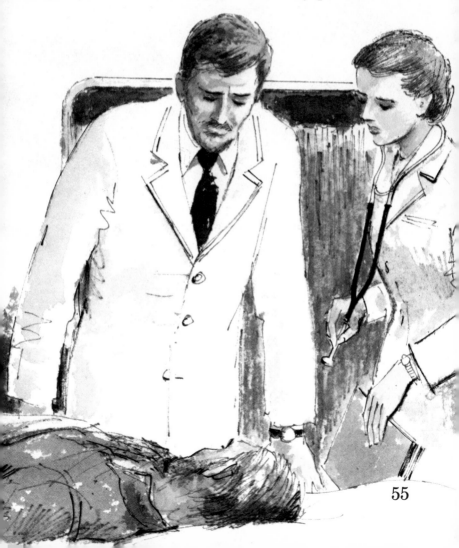

animals. By using a piece of cloth as a strainer, plankton can be lifted from the water.

Now Bombard was ready to test his ideas. He would cross the Atlantic, living as a shipwreck victim. His friends begged him not to do it. "You have made your point, Alain. Why risk your life this way?"

Bombard's answer came quickly. "It is to sailors that I must prove what I say, for they

risk their lives every day. I must show them a person can stay alive for weeks by using the sea itself and the life in it."

Bombard had a special rubber life raft made. It had a small sail and held a few tools, but it had no food or water. On the first night out, huge waves began to wash over the raft. The storm lasted for six days. During that time, Bombard ate nothing and drank only seawater. Finally he tied his knife to an oar and speared a fish with it. The fish juice helped his need for water, and the fish meat gave him food.

He found ways to make do with what he had on the raft. He used his hat to toss out water that got into his raft. A piece of rubber was shaped into a *funnel* (cone) to catch rainwater. A fishbone was now a fishhook.

Each day Bombard did half an hour of exercises so his body would not get weak. Each day he checked himself from head to toe to see what his sea journey was doing to him. All his findings were noted in a book. Often Bombard lost his way. His book shows that he almost lost hope, too. "The raft will reach port, but I will be dead in it."

When he reached Barbados, he had lost 88 pounds (40 kilograms). He was sick—but he was alive!

Today, thanks to Bombard, thousands of people who might have died at sea are still alive. Sailors of many countries have learned how to live through shipwrecks by following Bombard's example. Special life rafts like his are carried on hundreds of big ships. They are called *bombards* in his honor. In the

bombards are things like plankton nets and fishing lines.

People still write to Bombard to thank him for making his brave journey. Two people were shipwrecked in the Pacific Ocean. They lived for five weeks on a raft by drinking only seawater and fish juice. They know what they owe to Bombard. "Bombard's action made our raft a lifesaver instead of a grave."

SIMPLE THINGS   *supporting details*

Complete each sentence by writing the
numeral of the missing word or words
underneath in the blanks.

1. knife tied to an oar
2. hat
3. Vitamin C
4. fresh water
5. a piece of rubber
6. fishhook

Bombard used his ___ to toss out
water.
He made a spear from a ___.
He turned a fishbone into a ___.
To catch rainwater, he used a funnel
made from ___.
Plankton gave him ___.
He used fish to get food and ___.

🔑 *210 • Best Score 6 • My Score* ___

WHAT DO THEY MEAN?   *sentence meaning*

Each main sentence below is followed by two
sentences. Circle the letter of one of the two
sentences underneath that best tells you the
meaning of the main sentence.

1. *The idea had begun to take root in
Bombard's mind at least a year before.*
    a. Bombard had been thinking about
       carrying out his idea for a year.

b. The idea was like a weed that took root and choked off other ideas.

2. *Bombard looked into the records.*
   a. Bombard read reports.
   b. Bombard played records.

3. *Bombard's friends said to him, "You have made your point, Alain."*
   a. You already scored a point.
   b. You have already shown that your idea is a good one.

4. *The people who were shipwrecked in the Pacific Ocean said, "Bombard's action made our raft a life saver instead of a grave."*
   a. After hearing about Bombard, we made a raft to save the lives of people who were shipwrecked.
   b. By learning from the things Bombard did to stay alive, we were able to stay alive.

☞86 · *Best Score 4 · My Score* _____
All Best Scores 10 · All My Scores _____

SAVING A LIFE   *values*

If you had been one of Bombard's friends, would you have told him to go to sea or to stay home? Give reasons for your answer.

They Take Snapshots

Key Words

snapshots
microphone
record, recording

in Sound *by Peter Browne*

What does an ant sound like when it's eating? A girl in France found out by using a tape recorder. She put the microphone on an anthill. The munching sounds of an ant eating are like the sound of a person crunching on toast.

The French girl is one of many sound lovers who are making snapshots in sound. A small tape recorder is like a small camera. It can be carried in a coat pocket. When the sound hunter comes across an interesting sound, out comes the recorder, and on goes the *record* button.

The sound might be the honks of horns in a traffic jam. Or it might be the peal of church bells. It could be the voices of young people singing in a park.

Some hunters also go seeking special sounds. One person attended a trombone players' meeting. The result was a recording of 1200 trombones being blown at one time. But it can take a long time to find a certain sound. How many people would wait a year for the sound of the <u>perfect</u> thunderstorm?

A sound hunter learns how to deal with many sounds. He or she combines them to create a single recording. Once, 16 talking

parrots were the speakers. Their words were put together. It seemed as if they were chatting with one another.

A man in Denmark used animal stars, too. He drove from farm to farm to record the barks of 17 different kinds of dogs. As he listened to the tapes, he wondered if the barks could be put together to make a tune.

He chose five types of barks. Barks from small dogs were used for the high notes. The deep woofs of big dogs were used for low notes. The sound hunter recorded them several times. He labored for a week with scissors and tape. The result of his hard work was "Oh, Susannah." Later he made a record. On it, dogs seem to bark-sing "Pat-a-Cake," "Jingle Bells," "Three Blind Mice" and other tunes.

Some sound hunters have worked with tape to copy sounds few people will ever hear. There are tapes of a frozen lake. You can hear the sharp sounds of the thick ice as it shifts and cracks. There are tapes of dead wood. It makes buzzing thumping sounds as it dries.

A science teacher made a very unusual recording. It traces the sounds of life in an egg before it hatches. First there is the beat of the chick's heart. The beat grows stronger. Then there are the first few taps of the beak on the shell. The tapping becomes a knocking. The shell begins to crack with a sound like breaking glass. The chick gives a loud, happy cheep as the shell finally breaks open.

Sound hunters in different countries get to know about each other. Through the mail, they become "tapespondents." They talk to each other on tape across thousands of miles. They also exchange tapes.

Dick Kenny of Connecticut is a well-known tapespondent. He calls himself the Crazy Tapeworm. In his library of 2000 tapes, Kenny has the sound of a desert breeze, the rumble of a toadfish and the squeal of a San Francisco cable car. The Crazy Tapeworm shares these tapes with 89 tapespondents in 25 nations.

Right now Kenny is looking for a tape of a mouse eating cheese. Sound hunters may be working on it. Somewhere in the world, a mouse is about to put its head out of a hole. It will come out to nibble—and find itself facing a tiny microphone!

THAT SOUNDS LIKE . . . *comparison/contrast*

The author helped you picture or hear something by telling you what it was like. Complete the sentences below by writing the numerals of the endings in the blanks.

An ant eating is like ____.
A tape recorder is like ____.
An eggshell cracking is like ____.

1. a person crunching on toast
2. a camera
3. breaking glass

☞55 · *Best Score 3 · My Score* ____

WHAT SORT OF SOUND? *figurative language*

Read the phrases below. What other words could the author have used in place of the ones that are underlined? Write the numerals in the blanks.

1. screech
2. toots
3. barks
4. ringing

____ squeal of a San Francisco cable car
____ honks of horns in a traffic jam
____ deep woofs of big dogs
____ peal of church bells

☞104 · *Best Score 4 · My Score* ____

SOUND HUNTERS *summary*

Check (✔) the three sentences that sum up
the most important ideas in the article.

Sound hunters . . .

_____ 1. have an interesting hobby.

_____ 2. don't touch or change their tapes.

_____ 3. use only large tape recorders because
they want the best sound.

_____ 4. always wait for sounds to come to
them.

_____ 5. will go to a lot of time and trouble to
get a perfect new sound.

_____ 6. love to share their recordings with
other people.

_____ 7. like animals.

☞ *82 • Best Score 3 • My Score _____*

BE A SOUND HUNTER *sensory awareness*

Close your eyes and listen to the sounds
around you. Name as many as you can hear.

Key Words

garage
squawking
curious

Too Much of a Good Thing

by Will Stanton

Umm-umm! Chicken and gravy! That was one dish I could never get enough of. Or so I thought!

I read an ad in the newspaper one evening. "Hey, Maggie, here's a store selling chickens for a dollar each. That's much less than we'd pay elsewhere. I'm going to phone the store and order a dozen."

My wife stared at me. "What will we do with 12 chickens?"

"Cook them and freeze them. I can just see us on some chilly winter's night. We'll want to cook a chicken, and there it will be."

70

I called the store, and they said they would deliver the chickens the following day. When I got home that afternoon, the garage doors were shut. Two dogs and a cat were sniffing at the cracks under the doors.

Maggie pointed to the garage. "Some cold winter's night, we'll want a chicken, and there it will be."

I opened the garage doors and saw chickens everywhere, all of them alive! They were odd-looking chickens, too—red, yellow, blue and green. They had tried to squeeze themselves onto a shelf filled with paint cans.

71

The shelf had crashed to the floor, and the paint had splattered onto the chickens. There were feathers and paint every place I looked.

I put on some old clothes and started cramming chickens into the trunk of the car. After a lot of squawking and flapping, all the chickens were in. I slammed the trunk shut and sped away.

A few hours later, I was back. Maggie was curious. "What did you do with the chickens?"

"Gave them to a family in the country."

"Oh? What did they say?"

I grinned and said, "I don't know, Maggie. Nobody was home."

A week or so afterward, my friend Mac was helping me change the tires on my car. He opened the trunk and then stared down at the red, green, yellow and blue chicken tracks. He didn't utter a word.

I cleared my throat. "I was taking some chickens out to the country, but the paint wasn't dry."

Mac gave me a funny look. I didn't even try to explain.

There's an old saying: "You can't have too much of a good thing." But now I know it's not true. You <u>can</u> have too much—when it comes to chickens!

GETTING IT STRAIGHT   *sequence*

For each pair of sentences, circle the numeral of the one that tells you what happened first.

1. The store people brought the chickens.
2. Will phoned the store.

1. The chickens spilled the paint.
2. Will looked in the garage.

1. Mac helped Will change the tires.
2. Will drove the chickens to the country.

☞ 45 • *Best Score 3* • *My Score* _____

BIRD WORDS   *vocabulary*

Check (✔) the three words the author used to describe his chickens.

_____ 1. curious   _____ 4. odd-looking
_____ 2. flapping   _____ 5. squawking
_____ 3. sniffing

☞ 77 • *Best Score 3* • *My Score* _____

HINTS FROM THE AUTHOR   *author's purpose*

Circle the letter of the sentence that answers each question.

How do you know that . . .
Maggie is a person who thinks ahead?
    a. She sold the chickens to someone else.

    b. She asked Will, "What will we do
       with a dozen chickens?"
    c. She told Will to take the chickens to
       the country.

Will and Maggie have a phone?
    a. The ringing of the phone woke them.
    b. The chicken store owner called them.
    c. Will called up the store selling
       chickens.

Mac was surprised to see chicken tracks in the
trunk?
    a. He stared at them.
    b. He gave a yell.
    c. He asked Will about them.

Will was nervous when Mac saw the tracks.
    a. Will bit his nails.
    b. Will cleared his throat.
    c. Will's hands shook.

☞90 • Best Score 4 • My Score ____
All Best Scores 10 • All My Scores ____

_____

THINK THINGS THROUGH   *comparison/contrast*

Will Stanton thought that the chickens
would be dead and ready for cooking. When
have you taken something for granted when
you shouldn't have?

Key Words

scales, carp
silk

Fish Pictures

*by Masaya
Kusuhara*

"Oh, come on! No fish could be <u>that</u> big!"
Almost everyone who goes fishing has
heard or said those words. In Japan some
people keep special pictures of the fish they
catch. The pictures are made through
Gyotaku (jo-TAH-koo), or *fish printing.*

*The fish is spread with
different-colored inks.*

*The artist places
paper over the fish.*

A fish print shows the size of the fish. It also outlines the scales, fins and eye. It shows the beauty and strength of a large fish like the carp. But a fish print has its own special touch, too. The fish is shown in bright colors—any colors the fisher-artist chooses.

To make a print, the Gyotaku artist first washes the fish and pats it dry. Now the artist can go ahead in either of two ways. In the first way, the artist spreads different-colored inks thinly and evenly over the fish and then places paper over it. The artist rubs the paper from head to tail and gently lifts the paper. And there is the print!

The artist rubs the paper.

The artist lifts the paper, and there is the print.

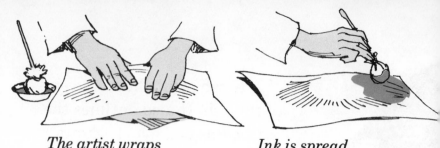

*The artist wraps
the fish.*

*Ink is spread
over the paper.*

In the second way of making a fish print, the artist wraps the fish in paper. Then he or she spreads ink over the paper instead of over the fish. The artist does not use fingers to spread the colors. Instead, he or she places the ink on a piece of cotton covered with silk. The artist rubs this silk-cotton ball over the paper. The print can look like a delicate Japanese painting.

A Gyotaku artist can add finishing touches to a print. Fine lines can be drawn to point up interesting shapes and forms on the fish's body. But one Gyotaku artist added too many finishing touches.

The fisher submitted a print in a contest for the longest fish caught that year. The judges looked at Gyotaku prints to search for the winner. The fish shown in that fisher's print seemed to have a strangely pointed mouth. Was this some new sort of sea

The artist lifts the paper from the fish.

The artist adds finishing touches.

creature? No. The fisher-artist had wrapped paper over the other side of the fish's mouth, too. In this way, the fish looked longer.

There are Gyotaku prints that show <u>really</u> big fish. One person used a bedsheet to make a print of a large shark. Another artist made a print of an even larger fish.

This print was made on silk.

Some people are using Gyotaku to make prints of other kinds of ocean life. There are Gyotaku prints of lobsters, octopuses, seaweed, starfish, corals and crabs.

Perhaps the most joyful print of all shows 70 fish of 14 different kinds. Large and small, they seem to dance across the huge piece of cloth. In their bright colors and clear shapes, they are like some fisher's happy dream of a perfect day on the ocean.

THE ARTIST AT WORK   *sequence*

One way of making a fish print is listed below.
Write the numerals of the steps in the correct
order in the fish print underneath.

The artist . . .

1. places paper over the inked fish.
2. rubs the paper.
3. washes the fish and pats it dry.
4. takes off the paper with the fish print
   on it.
5. spreads the ink over the fish.

WHAT DO YOU SEE? *supporting details*

Circle the numerals of the three things you can see when you look at a fish print.

1. speed
2. size
3. insides

4. color
5. growth
6. scales

☞ *83 • Best Score 3 • My Score* _____

A JOYFUL DANCE *paragraph meaning*

Read the last paragraph in the article. Underline the letters of the two best answers to the question below.

Why does the author call this fish print joyful?

a. There are 70 fish.
b. The colors are bright and clear.
c. The cloth is huge.
d. The fish seem to dance across the cloth.

☞ *21 • Best Score 2 • My Score* _____

All Best Scores 10 • All My Scores _____

MAKE AN IMPRESSION *graphics*

Which of the two ways would you use to make a fish print? How would you add finishing touches to your print?

Cowhands of the Deep

by Lord Ritchie-Calder

Key Words

cattle
herd
dolphins
pastures
power stations
filter

One by one, the cowhands got up from their beds and got ready for another day of herding the ranch's animals. After breakfast they pulled on their gear and swam outside.

Swam? Yes, for these aren't cowhands of the old Wild West. They are cowhands of the future. And they won't ride the range. They will swim the sea.

The oceans hold great numbers of fish. Many people say that in the future these fish may be like the cattle and sheep of today. Underwater ranch hands would herd their animals in the same way. Some people think that dolphins could be trained like sheep dogs to watch over the fish.

The schools of fish would be driven to pastures of sea plants. The fish would live on these plants, and later the fish would be caught as food for people. In fact, the sea plants themselves could be grown and used as food for human beings the way spinach and other plants are. Fish could be kept all year round. The water could even be heated. Right now many power stations pump in cold water to cool their engines. Then they pump out the water, which is now hot. This once-useless hot water could warm the fish farms.

There are tiny sea creatures called *krill*. They live with and eat the sea plants. Krill taste like shrimp and are the baleen whale's only food. The whale gulps up huge mouthfuls of water in which krill float. The whale wants only the krill, not the water. So it shoots the water back into the sea. As the

The whale takes in large amounts of water and krill.

The whale shoots the water back into the sea. Krill are trapped in the baleen.

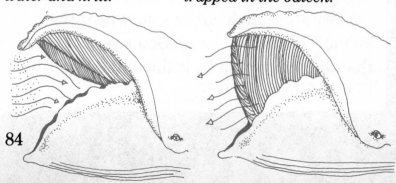

water leaves the whale's mouth, it passes through the whale's baleen. Baleen is like a filter made of strands of soft bone. The krill are trapped in the baleen and are eaten by the whale.

Some people say that we can learn from the baleen whale. Someday there may be a human-made whale that could scoop up and strain this "krill soup" and turn it into a food fit for people.

Crazy ideas? Many scientists think they are ideas that have a good chance of becoming real. In fact, one country has used the hot water from a power station to heat a fish farm. Perhaps food from the sea to feed the world is not too far away.

FISH TANK *comparison/contrast*

Each of the things listed in the fish tank below is compared to one of the items in the column at the right. Write the letter of each thing from the sea on the line next to its matching land term.

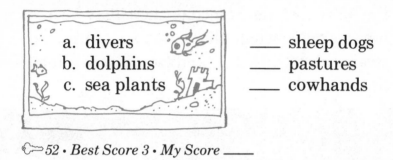

a. divers
b. dolphins
c. sea plants

____ sheep dogs
____ pastures
____ cowhands

🔑 52 · *Best Score 3 · My Score* ____

EATING LIKE A WHALE *sequence*

The steps the baleen whale uses to eat krill are listed below, but they are out of order. List the numbers of these steps in the correct order on the lines in the whale on the next page.

1. The baleen traps the krill inside the whale's mouth.
2. The whale eats the krill.
3. The whale blows the water out through its mouth.
4. The whale takes in a mouthful of water.

86

A FISH STORY? *fact/opinion*

Some things in the article are facts. Others are just ideas for what might happen in the future. Put 1 in front of each fact and 2 in front of each sentence that is just an idea.

___ There are lots of fish in the ocean.
___ Dolphins could be trained to herd fish.
___ There is a power station whose hot water can heat a fish farm.

IDEAS AS BIG AS THE SEA *projecting*

Which, if any, of the ideas in the article do you think are likely to happen? Why? What ideas do you have for using the sea to help people?

Key Words

insane asylum
patients
mentally ill
legislatures
dedicated

And She Brought Them Light

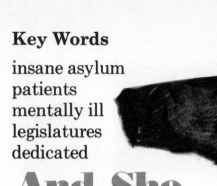

by Stewart H. Holbrook

Dorothea Dix turned to the woman in charge of the insane asylum and asked, "Do you have any other patients?"

The woman said, "Yes, we have one more. His name is Abraham Simmons, but you can't go into his cell. He'll kill you if you get near him."

"Please," said Dorothea, "let me see where he is."

"All right, but wait here until I get a lantern."

Dorothea waited by a stone building that stood in the courtyard. In a few minutes, the woman returned with the lantern.

Dorothea followed her into a dark hall. At the end rose a heavy iron door. The woman fitted the key into the lock and opened the door a few inches. The odor from inside was so bad that Dorothea had to go outside for air to breathe. Then she went back. The woman pushed open the door again and led Dorothea inside.

Dorothea could scarcely believe what she saw. A man with ragged, dirty hair faced them. His ribs showed, for he didn't get much to eat. No one had given him any shoes. He stood on the cold, damp stone floor in his bare feet. A big chain ran from some heavy iron bars on the floor, around one of his legs and up to the ceiling.

Dorothea looked around the room. It was very small. There wasn't even much room for the man to stand up or to lie down. There were no windows in the cell. The man had to live in total darkness. The only people he ever saw were the woman and her husband.

Dorothea quietly walked up to the man, took his icy hands in hers and started speaking to him. She tried to warm his hands by rubbing them with her own.

"Please get away from him," begged the woman, "or he'll kill you."

But Dorothea did not listen to her. She went on talking to the man, trying to make him answer. Abraham Simmons just stood where he was. He did not say one word, nor did he move. But Dorothea must have gotten through to him, for a single tear rolled down his cheek.

As Dorothea and the woman shut the cell door behind them, the woman spoke. "He didn't even try to hurt you! Sometimes he just screams and screams. That's the reason we have double walls and doors in the building. We don't want to hear his cries when we're in the house. You know, sometimes when my husband goes to that cell on a winter morning, the walls are covered with frost. But that crazy man never shows any sign of freezing."

"How long has Mr. Simmons been there?" asked Dorothea.

"More than three years. We had him in a cage at first, but he escaped. So we had that special stone prison built. He can't get out of there!"

Dorothea Dix was angry about the way Abraham Simmons had to live. So she wrote a newspaper report about her experience. People all over the United States came to

recognize Simmons' name. As a result, the
state of Rhode Island passed new, more
humane laws. It wanted to make sure mental
patients were treated better.

   Dorothea Dix was perhaps the one
person who did the most to change people's
ideas about the mentally ill. She was born in
1802. She lived until 1887. In those times,
people who had mental problems were not
thought of as ill. The world called them
"insane" or "crazy" and forgot they were
human beings. So the people who took care of
them were not trying to be mean when they
treated their patients the way Abraham

Simmons was treated. The caretakers just did not know any better.

Dorothea saw many mentally ill people in her lifetime. Sometimes they were kept in jails, closets, cellars and cages. They often had little food to eat and wore torn, dirty clothes or even nothing at all. Few had heat in winter.

The more Dorothea Dix saw, the more she fought to improve things for these people. She thought that doctors and nurses should run things. She wanted the asylums to be hospitals, not prisons. She gave speeches. She wrote newspaper articles. She talked to state legislatures to have laws revised.

Not everyone agreed with Dorothea's way of thinking. Many did not like her. They said a woman's place was in the home. She shouldn't be visiting asylums. She should stop writing articles and making speeches. The

people in charge of the asylums and some of those in the legislatures hated her. Dorothea made them look bad when she spoke out. She showed that they were failing to do a good job.

Dorothea was dedicated to helping the mentally ill. She spent 20 years traveling. She went all over the United States and Canada.

Then the Civil War began in 1861. She put aside her work with the mentally ill. It was time to help the wounded soldiers. She was made the first Superintendent of Women Nurses.

When the war ended in 1865, she went back to helping the mentally ill. She did not stop until her death at 85 years of age.

WORDS SPEAK *comparison/contrast*

The words below on the left were words used by most people of the 1800s. The words on the right are used today. Write the letter of each word on the right next to the word on the left that means almost the same thing.

1800s	1900s
____ crazy	a. mentally ill
____ cell	b. room
____ insane asylum	c. hospital

☞49 · *Best Score 3 · My Score* ____

A SHOW OF CHARACTER *characterization*

Circle the letter of the word that best describes what kind of person Dorothea Dix was in each case below.

1. Dorothea had been warned that Abraham Simmons might kill her. But when she saw him, she quietly walked up to him.
   a. brave   b. sad   c. dazed

2. She took Simmons' icy hands in hers and tried to warm them by rubbing them with her own.
   a. proud   b. scared   c. kind

3. She spent over 40 years fighting for the mentally ill.
   a. dull   b. funny   c. dedicated

95

4. She wrote for newspapers and gave speeches.

    a. lazy b. intelligent c. liked sports

⚷89 · Best Score 4 · My Score _____

SETTING THE MOOD   *story elements*

Check (✔) the three sentences below that tell how the author created a feeling of danger and mystery at the beginning of the article.

_____ 1. He used the words "insane asylum."

_____ 2. He told you that Dorothea was the first Superintendent of Women Nurses.

_____ 3. He described what people of the 1800s thought about the mentally ill.

_____ 4. The building was made of cold stone and had a dark hall with a heavy iron door.

_____ 5. The woman carefully opened the door.

⚷76 · Best Score 3 · My Score _____

All Best Scores 10 · All My Scores _____

DOROTHEA TODAY   *predicting*

If Dorothea Dix were alive today, what problems do you think she would write about and try to change? Give reasons for your answer.